Want... ...sy
on... ...8
sty... ...llection from Melissa
Leapman are surprisingly easy to crochet.

Contents

LEISURE ARTS, INC. • Maumelle, Arkansas

SHOPPING LIST

Yarn (Medium Weight) 🧶**4**
[3.5 ounces, 202 yards
(100 grams, 185 meters) per skein]:
☐ 5 skeins

Crochet Hook

☐ Size H (5 mm)
   or size needed for gauge

Sparkle

Finished Size: 58" (147.5 cm) wide

●●○○ **EASY**

GAUGE INFORMATION

16 dc and 8 rows = 4" (10 cm)

Gauge Swatch: 4" (10 cm) square

Ch 18.

Row 1: Dc in fourth ch from hook (3 skipped chs count as first dc) and in each ch across: 16 dc.

Rows 2-8: Ch 3 (**counts as first dc**), turn; dc in next dc and in each dc across.

Finish off.

WRAP

Row 1 (Right side)**:** Beginning at top edge, use an adjustable loop to form a ring *(Figs. 1a-d, page 30)*, ch 3 (**counts as first dc, now and throughout**), 6 dc in ring: 7 dc.

Row 2: Ch 4 (**counts as first dc plus ch 1, now and throughout**), turn; dc in next dc, (ch 1, dc in next dc) across: 7 dc and 6 ch-1 sps.

Row 3: Ch 3, turn; (2 dc in next ch-1 sp, dc in next dc) across: 19 dc.

Row 4: Ch 4, turn; dc in next dc, ch 1, skip next dc, ★ (dc in next dc, ch 1) twice, skip next dc; repeat from ★ across to last dc, dc in last dc: 13 dc and 12 ch-1 sps.

Row 5: Ch 3, turn; dc in first dc and in next ch-1 sp, dc in next dc and in next ch-1 sp, ★ 2 dc in next dc, dc in next ch-1 sp, dc in next dc and in next ch-1 sp; repeat from ★ across to last dc, dc in last dc: 31 dc.

Row 6: Ch 4, turn; dc in next dc, (ch 1, skip next dc, dc in next dc) twice, ★ ch 1, dc in next dc, (ch 1, skip next dc, dc in next dc) twice; repeat from ★ across: 19 dc and 18 ch-1 sps.

Row 7: Ch 3, turn; dc in first dc and next ch-1 sp, (dc in next dc and in next ch-1 sp) twice, ★ 2 dc in next dc, dc in next ch-1 sp, (dc in next dc and in next ch-1 sp) twice; repeat from ★ across to last dc, dc in last dc: 43 dc.

Row 8: Ch 4, turn; dc in next dc, (ch 1, skip next dc, dc in next dc) 3 times, ★ ch 1, dc in next dc, (ch 1, skip next dc, dc in next dc) 3 times; repeat from ★ across: 25 dc and 24 ch-1 sps.

Row 9: Ch 3, turn; dc in first dc and in next ch-1 sp, (dc in next dc and in next ch-1 sp) 3 times, ★ 2 dc in next dc, dc in next ch-1 sp, (dc in next dc and in next ch-1 sp) 3 times; repeat from ★ across to last dc, dc in last dc: 55 dc.

Row 10: Ch 4, turn; dc in next dc, (ch 1, skip next dc, dc in next dc) 4 times, ★ ch 1, dc in next dc, (ch 1, skip next dc, dc in next dc) 4 times; repeat from ★ across: 31 dc and 30 ch-1 sps.

Row 11: Ch 3, turn; dc in first dc and in next ch-1 sp, (dc in next dc and in next ch-1 sp) 4 times, ★ 2 dc in next dc, dc in next ch-1 sp, (dc in next dc and in next ch-1 sp) 4 times; repeat from ★ across to last dc, dc in last dc: 67 dc.

Row 12: Ch 4, turn; dc in next dc, (ch 1, skip next dc, dc in next dc) 5 times, ★ ch 1, dc in next dc, (ch 1, skip next dc, dc in next dc) 5 times; repeat from ★ across: 37 dc and 36 ch-1 sps.

Row 13: Ch 3, turn; dc in first dc and in next ch-1 sp, (dc in next dc and in next ch-1 sp) 5 times, ★ 2 dc in next dc, dc in next ch-1 sp, (dc in next dc and in next ch-1 sp) 5 times; repeat from ★ across to last dc, dc in last dc: 79 dc.

Row 14: Ch 4, turn; dc in next dc, (ch 1, skip next dc, dc in next dc) 6 times, ★ ch 1, dc in next dc, (ch 1, skip next dc, dc in next dc) 6 times; repeat from ★ across: 43 dc and 42 ch-1 sps.

Row 15: Ch 3, turn; dc in first dc and in next ch-1 sp, (dc in next dc and in next ch-1 sp) 6 times, ★ 2 dc in next dc, dc in next ch-1 sp, (dc in next dc and in next ch-1 sp) 6 times; repeat from ★ across to last dc, dc in last dc: 91 dc.

Row 16: Ch 4, turn; dc in next dc, (ch 1, skip next dc, dc in next dc) 7 times, ★ ch 1, dc in next dc, (ch 1, skip next dc, dc in next dc) 7 times; repeat from ★ across: 49 dc and 48 ch-1 sps.

Row 17: Ch 3, turn; dc in first dc and in next ch-1 sp, (dc in next dc and in next ch-1 sp) 7 times, ★ 2 dc in next dc, dc in next ch-1 sp, (dc in next dc and in next ch-1 sp) 7 times; repeat from ★ across to last dc, dc in last dc: 103 dc.

Row 18: Ch 4, turn; dc in next dc, (ch 1, skip next dc, dc in next dc) 8 times, ★ ch 1, dc in next dc, (ch 1, skip next dc, dc in next dc) 8 times; repeat from ★ across: 55 dc and 54 ch-1 sps.

Row 19: Ch 3, turn; dc in first dc and in next ch-1 sp, (dc in next dc and in next ch-1 sp) 8 times, ★ 2 dc in next dc, dc in next ch-1 sp, (dc in next dc and in next ch-1 sp) 8 times; repeat from ★ across to last dc, dc in last dc: 115 dc.

Row 20: Ch 4, turn; dc in next dc, (ch 1, skip next dc, dc in next dc) 9 times, ★ ch 1, dc in next dc, (ch 1, skip next dc, dc in next dc) 9 times; repeat from ★ across: 61 dc and 60 ch-1 sps.

Row 21: Ch 3, turn; dc in first dc and in next ch-1 sp, (dc in next dc and in next ch-1 sp) 9 times, ★ 2 dc in next dc, dc in next ch-1 sp, (dc in next dc and in next ch-1 sp) 9 times; repeat from ★ across to last dc, dc in last dc: 127 dc.

Row 22: Ch 4, turn; dc in next dc, (ch 1, skip next dc, dc in next dc) 10 times, ★ ch 1, dc in next dc, (ch 1, skip next dc, dc in next dc) 10 times; repeat from ★ across: 67 dc and 66 ch-1 sps.

Row 23: Ch 3, turn; dc in first dc and in next ch-1 sp, (dc in next dc and in next ch-1 sp) 10 times, ★ 2 dc in next dc, dc in next ch-1 sp, (dc in next dc and in next ch-1 sp) 10 times; repeat from ★ across to last dc, dc in last dc: 139 dc.

Row 24: Ch 4, turn; dc in next dc, (ch 1, skip next dc, dc in next dc) 11 times, ★ ch 1, dc in next dc, (ch 1, skip next dc, dc in next dc) 11 times; repeat from ★ across: 73 dc and 72 ch-1 sps.

Row 25: Ch 3, turn; dc in first dc and in next ch-1 sp, (dc in next dc and in next ch-1 sp) 11 times, ★ 2 dc in next dc, dc in next ch-1 sp, (dc in next dc and in next ch-1 sp) 11 times; repeat from ★ across to last dc, dc in last dc: 151 dc.

Row 26: Ch 4, turn; dc in next dc, (ch 1, skip next dc, dc in next dc) 12 times, ★ ch 1, dc in next dc, (ch 1, skip next dc, dc in next dc) 12 times; repeat from ★ across: 79 dc and 78 ch-1 sps.

Row 27: Ch 3, turn; dc in first dc and in next ch-1 sp, (dc in next dc and in next ch-1 sp) 12 times, ★ 2 dc in next dc, dc in next ch-1 sp, (dc in next dc and in next ch-1 sp) 12 times; repeat from ★ across to last dc, dc in last dc: 163 dc.

Row 28: Ch 4, turn; dc in next dc, (ch 1, skip next dc, dc in next dc) 13 times, ★ ch 1, dc in next dc, (ch 1, skip next dc, dc in next dc) 13 times; repeat from ★ across: 85 dc and 84 ch-1 sps.

Row 29: Ch 3, turn; dc in first dc and in next ch-1 sp, (dc in next dc and in next ch-1 sp) 13 times, ★ 2 dc in next dc, dc in next ch-1 sp, (dc in next dc and in next ch-1 sp) 13 times; repeat from ★ across to last dc, dc in last dc: 175 dc.

Row 30: Ch 4, turn; dc in next dc, (ch 1, skip next dc, dc in next dc) 14 times, ★ ch 1, dc in next dc, (ch 1, skip next dc, dc in next dc) 14 times; repeat from ★ across: 91 dc and 90 ch-1 sps.

Row 31: Ch 3, turn; dc in first dc and in next ch-1 sp, (dc in next dc and in next ch-1 sp) 14 times, ★ 2 dc in next dc, dc in next ch-1 sp, (dc in next dc and in next ch-1 sp) 14 times; repeat from ★ across to last dc, dc in last dc: 187 dc.

Row 32: Ch 4, turn; dc in next dc, (ch 1, skip next dc, dc in next dc) 15 times, ★ ch 1, dc in next dc, (ch 1, skip next dc, dc in next dc) 15 times; repeat from ★ across: 97 dc and 96 ch-1 sps.

Row 33: Ch 3, turn; dc in first dc and in next ch-1 sp, (dc in next dc and in next ch-1 sp) 15 times, ★ 2 dc in next dc, dc in next ch-1 sp, (dc in next dc and in next ch-1 sp) 15 times; repeat from ★ across to last dc, dc in last dc: 199 dc.

Row 34: Ch 4, turn; dc in next dc, (ch 1, skip next dc, dc in next dc) 16 times, ★ ch 1, dc in next dc, (ch 1, skip next dc, dc in next dc) 16 times; repeat from ★ across: 103 dc and 102 ch-1 sps.

Row 35: Ch 3, turn; dc in first dc and in next ch-1 sp, (dc in next dc and in next ch-1 sp) 16 times, ★ 2 dc in next dc, dc in next ch-1 sp, (dc in next dc and in next ch-1 sp) 16 times; repeat from ★ across to last dc, dc in last dc: 211 dc.

Row 36: Ch 4, turn; dc in next dc, (ch 1, skip next dc, dc in next dc) 17 times, ★ ch 1, dc in next dc, (ch 1, skip next dc, dc in next dc) 17 times; repeat from ★ across: 109 dc and 108 ch-1 sps.

Row 37: Ch 3, turn; dc in first dc and in next ch-1 sp, (dc in next dc and in next ch-1 sp) 17 times, ★ 2 dc in next dc, dc in next ch-1 sp, (dc in next dc and in next ch-1 sp) 17 times; repeat from ★ across to last dc, dc in last dc: 223 dc.

Row 38: Ch 4, turn; dc in next dc, (ch 1, skip next dc, dc in next dc) 18 times, ★ ch 1, dc in next dc, (ch 1, skip next dc, dc in next dc) 18 times; repeat from ★ across: 115 dc and 114 ch-1 sps.

Row 39: Ch 3, turn; dc in first dc and in next ch-1 sp, (dc in next dc and in next ch-1 sp) 18 times, ★ 2 dc in next dc, dc in next ch-1 sp, (dc in next dc and in next ch-1 sp) 18 times; repeat from ★ across to last dc, dc in last dc: 235 dc.

Row 40: Ch 4, turn; dc in next dc, (ch 1, skip next dc, dc in next dc) 19 times, ★ ch 1, dc in next dc, (ch 1, skip next dc, dc in next dc) 19 times; repeat from ★ across: 121 dc and 120 ch-1 sps.

Row 41: Ch 3, turn; dc in first dc and in next ch-1 sp, (dc in next dc and in next ch-1 sp) 19 times, ★ 2 dc in next dc, dc in next ch-1 sp, (dc in next dc and in next ch-1 sp) 19 times; repeat from ★ across to last dc, dc in last dc: 247 dc.

Row 42: Ch 4, turn; dc in next dc, (ch 1, skip next dc, dc in next dc) 20 times, ★ ch 1, dc in next dc, (ch 1, skip next dc, dc in next dc) 20 times; repeat from ★ across: 127 dc and 126 ch-1 sps.

Row 43: Ch 3, turn; dc in first dc and in next ch-1 sp, (dc in next dc and in next ch-1 sp) 20 times, ★ 2 dc in next dc, dc in next ch-1 sp, (dc in next dc and in next ch-1 sp) 20 times; repeat from ★ across to last dc, dc in last dc: 259 dc.

Row 44: Ch 4, turn; dc in next dc, (ch 1, skip next dc, dc in next dc) 21 times, ★ ch 1, dc in next dc, (ch 1, skip next dc, dc in next dc) 21 times; repeat from ★ across: 133 dc and 132 ch-1 sps.

Row 45: Ch 3, turn; dc in first dc and in next ch-1 sp, (dc in next dc and in next ch-1 sp) 21 times, ★ 2 dc in next dc, dc in next ch-1 sp, (dc in next dc and in next ch-1 sp) 21 times; repeat from ★ across to last dc, dc in last dc: 271 dc.

Row 46: Ch 4, turn; dc in next dc, (ch 1, skip next dc, dc in next dc) 22 times, ★ ch 1, dc in next dc, (ch 1, skip next dc, dc in next dc) 22 times; repeat from ★ across: 139 dc and 138 ch-1 sps.

Row 47: Ch 3, turn; dc in first dc and in next ch-1 sp, (dc in next dc and in next ch-1 sp) 22 times, ★ 2 dc in next dc, dc in next ch-1 sp, (dc in next dc and in next ch-1 sp) 22 times; repeat from ★ across to last dc, dc in last dc: 283 dc.

Row 48: Ch 4, turn; dc in next dc, (ch 1, skip next dc, dc in next dc) 23 times, ★ ch 1, dc in next dc, (ch 1, skip next dc, dc in next dc) 23 times; repeat from ★ across: 145 dc and 144 ch-1 sps.

Row 49: Ch 3, turn; dc in first dc and in next ch-1 sp, (dc in next dc and in next ch-1 sp) 23 times, ★ 2 dc in next dc, dc in next ch-1 sp, (dc in next dc and in next ch-1 sp) 23 times; repeat from ★ across to last dc, dc in last dc: 295 dc.

Row 50: Ch 4, turn; dc in next dc, (ch 1, skip next dc, dc in next dc) 24 times, ★ ch 1, dc in next dc, (ch 1, skip next dc, dc in next dc) 24 times; repeat from ★ across: 151 dc and 150 ch-1 sps.

Row 51: Ch 3, turn; dc in first dc and in next ch-1 sp, (dc in next dc and in next ch-1 sp) 24 times, ★ 2 dc in next dc, dc in next ch-1 sp, (dc in next dc and in next ch-1 sp) 24 times; repeat from ★ across to last dc, dc in last dc: 307 dc.

Row 52: Ch 4, turn; dc in next dc, (ch 1, skip next dc, dc in next dc) 25 times, ★ ch 1, dc in next dc, (ch 1, skip next dc, dc in next dc) 25 times; repeat from ★ across: 157 dc and 156 ch-1 sps.

Row 53: Ch 3, turn; dc in first dc and in next ch-1 sp, (dc in next dc and in next ch-1 sp) 25 times, ★ 2 dc in next dc, dc in next ch-1 sp, (dc in next dc and in next ch-1 sp) 25 times; repeat from ★ across to last dc, dc in last dc: 319 dc.

Row 54: Ch 4, turn; dc in next dc, (ch 1, skip next dc, dc in next dc) 26 times, ★ ch 1, dc in next dc, (ch 1, skip next dc, dc in next dc) 26 times; repeat from ★ across: 163 dc and 162 ch-1 sps.

Row 55: Ch 3, turn; dc in first dc and in next ch-1 sp, (dc in next dc and in next ch-1 sp) 26 times, ★ 2 dc in next dc, dc in next ch-1 sp, (dc in next dc and in next ch-1 sp) 26 times; repeat from ★ across to last dc, dc in last dc: 331 dc.

Row 56: Ch 4, turn; dc in next dc, (ch 1, skip next dc, dc in next dc) 27 times, ★ ch 1, dc in next dc, (ch 1, skip next dc, dc in next dc) 27 times; repeat from ★ across: 169 dc and 168 ch-1 sps.

Row 57: Ch 3, turn; dc in first dc and in next ch-1 sp, (dc in next dc and in next ch-1 sp) 27 times, ★ 2 dc in next dc, dc in next ch-1 sp, (dc in next dc and in next ch-1 sp) 27 times; repeat from ★ across to last dc, dc in last dc: 343 dc.

Row 58: Ch 4, turn; dc in next dc, (ch 1, skip next dc, dc in next dc) 28 times, ★ ch 1, dc in next dc, (ch 1, skip next dc, dc in next dc) 28 times; repeat from ★ across: 175 dc and 174 ch-1 sps.

Row 59: Ch 1, turn; slip st in first dc, ★ skip next ch-1 sp, dc in next dc, (ch 1, dc in same st) 4 times, skip next ch-1 sp, slip st in next dc; repeat from ★ across; do **not** finish off.

Edging: Ch 1, do **not** turn; sc evenly across ends of rows to beginning ring, sc in ring, sc evenly across ends of rows; slip st in first slip st on Row 59; finish off.

SHOPPING LIST

Yarn (Fine Weight) (2)
[1.75 ounces, 202 yards
(50 grams, 185 meters) per skein]:
☐ Purple - 4 skeins
☐ Wine - 1 skein
☐ Lt Grey - 1 skein
(Medium Weight) (4)
[3 ounces, 185 yards
(85 grams, 170 meters) per skein]:
☐ Grey - 2 skeins

Crochet Hook
☐ Size H (5 mm)
   or size needed for gauge

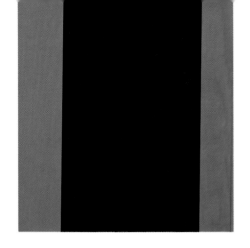

Shimmering Ripple

Finished Size: 70" long x 22" wide (178 cm x 56 cm)

●●○○ **EASY**

GAUGE INFORMATION

In pattern, one repeat

  (14 dc and 7 ch-1 sps) = 3½" (9 cm);

  6 rows = 4" (10 cm)

Gauge Swatch: 7" wide x 4" high

  (17.75 cm x 10 cm)

With Purple, ch 48.

Work same as Wrap for 6 rows: 28 dc and 14 ch-1 sps.

STITCH GUIDE

DOUBLE CROCHET 2 TOGETHER

  (abbreviated dc2tog)

  (uses 2 dc and one ch-1 sp)

YO, insert hook in ch-1 sp or dc indicated, YO and pull up a loop, YO and draw through 2 loops on hook, skip next dc, YO, insert hook in next dc or ch-1 sp, YO and pull up a loop, YO and draw through 2 loops on hook, YO and draw through all 3 loops on hook (**counts as one dc**).

STRIPE SEQUENCE

One row **each:** ★ Purple, Wine, Purple, Grey, Purple, Lt Grey; repeat from ★ for sequence.

WRAP

With Purple, ch 462.

Row 1 (Right side): Dc in fifth ch from hook, [skip next 2 chs, (dc, ch 1, dc) in next ch] twice, skip next 2 chs, dc in next ch, (ch 1, dc in same ch) 3 times, [skip next 2 chs, (dc, ch 1, dc) in next ch] twice, ★ skip next 2 chs, † YO, insert hook in next ch, YO and pull up a loop, YO and draw through 2 loops on hook, YO, skip next ch, insert hook in next ch, YO and pull up a loop, YO and draw through 2 loops on hook, YO and draw through all 3 loops on hook (**counts as one dc**) †; repeat from † to † once **more**, [skip next 2 chs, (dc, ch 1, dc) in next ch] twice, skip next 2 chs, dc in next ch, (ch 1, dc in same ch) 3 times, [skip next 2 chs, (dc, ch 1, dc) in next ch] twice; repeat from ★ across to last 5 chs, YO, skip next 2 chs, insert hook in next ch, YO and pull up a loop, YO and draw through 2 loops on hook, YO, skip next ch, insert hook in last ch, YO and pull up a loop, YO and draw through 2 loops on hook, cut old color, with next color (**Fig. 3, page 30**), YO and draw through all 3 loops on hook (**counts as last dc**): 280 dc and 140 ch-1 sps.

Row 2: Ch 2, turn; dc in next ch-1 sp, ★ † (dc, ch 1, dc) in each of next 2 ch-1 sps, dc in next ch-1 sp, (ch 1, dc in same sp) 3 times, (dc, ch 1, dc) in each of next 2 ch-1 sps, dc2tog beginning in next ch-1 sp †, dc2tog beginning in next dc; repeat from ★ 18 times **more**, then repeat from † to † once changing to next color in last dc2tog.

Following Stripe Sequence on page 9, repeat Row 2 for pattern until piece measures 22" (56 cm) from beginning ch, ending by working a **right** side (Purple) row; at end of last row, do **not** change colors, finish off.

Stepping Out

SHOPPING LIST

Yarn (Medium Weight) 4

[3.5 ounces, 186 yards
(100 grams, 170 meters) per skein]:

☐ Grey - 2 skeins

☐ Blue - 2 skeins

☐ Lt Blue - 1 skein

☐ Lt Grey - 1 skein

☐ Ecru - 1 skein

Crochet Hook

☐ Size H (5 mm)

or size needed for gauge

Finished Size: 81" long x 32" wide (205.5 cm x 81.5 cm)

 **EASY**

GAUGE INFORMATION

16 dc and 8 rows = 4" (10 cm)

Gauge Swatch: 4" (10 cm) square

With Ecru, ch 18.

Row 1: Dc in fourth ch from hook **(3 skipped chs counts as first dc)** and in each ch across: 16 dc.

Rows 2-8: Ch 3 **(counts as first dc)**, turn; dc in next dc and in each dc across.

Finish off.

WRAP

With Ecru, ch 5.

Row 1: (Dc, ch 1, dc) in fifth ch from hook **(4 skipped chs count as first dc plus ch 1)**: 3 dc and 2 ch-1 sps.

Row 2 (Right side)**:** Ch 3 **(counts as first dc, now and throughout)**, turn; dc in next ch-1 sp, 2 dc in next dc and in next ch-1 sp, dc in last dc: 7 dc.

Row 3: Ch 4 **(counts as first dc plus ch 1)**, turn; dc in next dc, ch 1, skip next dc, (dc in next dc, ch 1) twice, skip next dc, dc in last dc: 5 dc and 4 ch-1 sps.

Row 4: Ch 3, turn; (dc in next ch-1 sp and in next dc) twice, (2 dc in next ch-1 sp, dc in next dc) twice: 11 dc.

Row 5 (Decrease row)**:** Ch 4, turn; (dc in next dc, ch 1) twice, skip next dc, dc in next dc, ch 1, skip next dc, dc in next dc, leave remaining 4 dc unworked: 5 dc and 4 ch-1 sps.

Row 6: Ch 3, turn; (dc in next ch-1 sp and in next dc) twice, (2 dc in next ch-1 sp, dc in next dc) twice: 11 dc.

Row 7: Ch 4, turn; dc in next dc, ch 1, skip next dc, (dc in next dc, ch 1) twice, skip next dc, dc in next dc, (ch 1, skip next dc, dc in next dc) twice: 7 dc and 6 ch-1 sps.

Row 8: Ch 3, turn; (dc in next ch-1 sp and in next dc) 4 times, (2 dc in next ch-1 sp, dc in next dc) twice: 15 dc.

Row 9: Ch 4, turn; (dc in next dc, ch 1) twice, skip next dc, dc in next dc, ★ ch 1, skip next dc, dc in next dc; repeat from ★ across to last 4 dc, leave remaining 4 dc unworked: 7 dc and 6 ch-1 sps.

Row 10: Ch 3, turn; (dc in next ch-1 sp and in next dc) across to last 2 ch-1 sps, (2 dc in next ch-1 sp, dc in next dc) twice: 15 dc.

Row 11: Ch 4, turn; dc in next dc, ch 1, skip next dc, (dc in next dc, ch 1) twice, skip next dc, dc in next dc, ★ ch 1, skip next dc, dc in next dc; repeat from ★ across: 9 dc and 8 ch-1 sps.

Row 12: Ch 3, turn; (dc in next ch-1 sp and in next dc) across to last 2 ch-1 sps, (2 dc in next ch-1 sp, dc in next dc) twice: 19 dc.

Rows 13-24: Repeat Rows 9-12, 3 times, changing to Lt Grey in last dc on Row 24 *(Fig. 3, page 30)*: 31 dc.

Rows 25-48: Repeat Rows 9-12, 6 times changing to Lt Blue in last dc on Row 48: 55 dc.

Rows 49-72: Repeat Rows 9-12, 6 times changing to Blue in last dc on Row 72: 79 dc.

Rows 73-96: Repeat Rows 9-12, 6 times changing to Grey in last dc on Row 96: 103 dc.

Rows 97-120: Repeat Rows 9-12, 6 times: 127 dc.

Finish off.

SHOPPING LIST

Yarn (Light Weight) [3 LIGHT]

[3.5 ounces, 254 yards
(100 grams, 232 meters) per skein]:

☐ Teal - 3 skeins

☐ Brown - 1 skein

☐ Red - 1 skein

Crochet Hook

☐ Size H (5 mm)

or size needed for gauge

Pretty Picots

Finished Size: 67" wide (across top edge) x 22¾" deep (170 cm x 58 cm)

●●○○ **EASY**

GAUGE INFORMATION

In pattern, (2 dc, ch 1, 2 dc) 4 times
  and 7 rows = 4" (10 cm)
Gauge Swatch: 7½" long x 3" high
  (19 cm x 7.5 cm)
Work same as Wrap through Row 5: 11 sps.

STITCH GUIDE

TREBLE CROCHET *(abbreviated tr)*
YO twice, insert hook in sp indicated, YO and pull
a loop (4 loops on hook), (YO and draw through
2 loops on hook) 3 times.
CLUSTER (uses one sp)
★ YO, insert hook in sp indicated, YO and pull up a
loop, YO and draw through 2 loops on hook; repeat
from ★ 2 times **more**, YO and draw through all 4
loops on hook.
PICOT
Ch 3, slip st in third ch from hook.

WRAP

Row 1: With Teal and beginning at top edge, use an
adjustable loop to form a ring *(Figs. 1a-d, page 30)*, ch 5
(counts as first tr plus ch 1, now and throughout), work
(Cluster, ch 3, Cluster, ch 1, tr) in ring: 3 sps.

Row 2 (Right side)**:** Ch 5, turn; (2 dc, ch 1, 2 dc) in next
ch-1 sp, (sc, ch 4, sc) in next ch-3 sp, (2 dc, ch 1) twice in
last ch-1 sp, tr in same sp, leave last tr unworked **(now and
throughout)**: 5 sps.

Row 3: Ch 5, turn; sc in next ch-1 sp, ch 4, sc in next
ch-1 sp, ch 4, work (Cluster, ch 3, Cluster) in next ch-4 sp
(corner made), ch 4, sc in next ch-1 sp, ch 4, (sc, ch 1, tr) in
last ch-1 sp: 7 sps.

Row 4: Ch 5, turn; (2 dc, ch 1, 2 dc) in next ch-1sp, (2 dc,
ch 1, 2 dc) in each ch-4 sp across to next corner ch-3 sp,
(sc, ch 4, sc) in corner ch-3 sp, (2 dc, ch 1, 2 dc) in each
ch-4 sp across to last ch-1 sp, (2 dc, ch 1) twice in last
ch-1 sp, tr in same sp: 9 sps.

Row 5: Ch 5, turn; (sc in next ch-1 sp, ch 4) across to next
corner ch-4 sp, work (Cluster, ch 3, Cluster) in corner
ch-4 sp, ch 4, (sc in next ch-1 sp, ch 4) across to last ch-1 sp,
(sc, ch 1, tr) in last ch-1 sp: 11 sps.

Rows 6-36: Repeat Rows 4 and 5, 15 times; then repeat
Row 4 once **more**: 73 sps.

Row 37: Ch 5, turn; (sc in next ch-1 sp, ch 4) across to next corner ch-4 sp, work (Cluster, ch 3, Cluster) in corner ch-4 sp, ch 4, (sc in next ch-1 sp, ch 4) across to last ch-1 sp, (sc, ch 1, tr) in last ch-1 sp, changing to Brown in last tr *(Fig. 3, page 30)*: 75 sps.

Row 38: Ch 5, turn; dc in next ch-1 sp, (ch 1, dc in same sp) 4 times, ★ sc in next ch-4 sp, dc in next ch-4 sp, (ch 1, dc in same sp) 4 times; repeat from ★ across to next corner ch-3 sp, (sc, ch 4, sc) in corner ch-3 sp, † dc in next ch-4 sp, (ch 1, dc in same sp) 4 times, sc in next ch-4 sp †; repeat from † to † across to last ch-1 sp, (dc in last ch-1 sp, ch 1) 5 times, tr in same sp: 230 sts and 155 sps.

Row 39: Ch 5, turn; sc in next ch-1 sp, skip next 2 dc, dc in next dc, (ch 1, dc in same st) 4 times, ★ † sc in next sc, skip next 2 dc, dc in next dc, (ch 1, dc in same st) 4 times †; repeat from ★ across to next corner ch-4 sp, work Cluster in corner ch-4 sp, (ch 3, work Cluster in same sp) twice, skip next 2 dc, dc in next dc, (ch 1, dc in same st) 4 times, repeat from † to † across to last ch-1 sp, (sc, ch 1, tr) in last ch-1 sp changing to Red.

Row 40: Ch 7, turn; slip st in third ch from hook, dc in next ch-1 sp, ch 1, (dc in same sp, ch 1) twice, working **around** Row 39, sc in ch-1 sp **below** next sc, ch 1, skip next 2 dc, dc in next dc, (ch 1, dc in same dc) twice, work Picot, (dc in same dc, ch 1) 3 times, † working **around** last 2 rows, 2 sc in ch-4 sp 3 rows **below**, ch 1, skip next 2 dc, dc in next dc, (ch 1, dc in same dc) twice, work Picot, (dc in same dc, ch 1) 3 times †; repeat from † to † across to corner 3-Cluster group, 2 sc in next ch-3 sp, ch 1, dc in next Cluster (ch 1, dc in same st) twice, work Picot, (dc in same st, ch 1) 3 times, 2 sc in next ch-3 sp, ch 1, skip next 2 dc, dc in next dc, (ch 1, dc in same dc) twice, work Picot, (dc in same dc, ch 1) 3 times, repeat from † to † across to last sc, working **around** Row 39, sc in ch-1 sp **below** last sc, (ch 1, dc in last ch-1 sp) 3 times, work Picot, ch 1, tr in same sp; finish off.

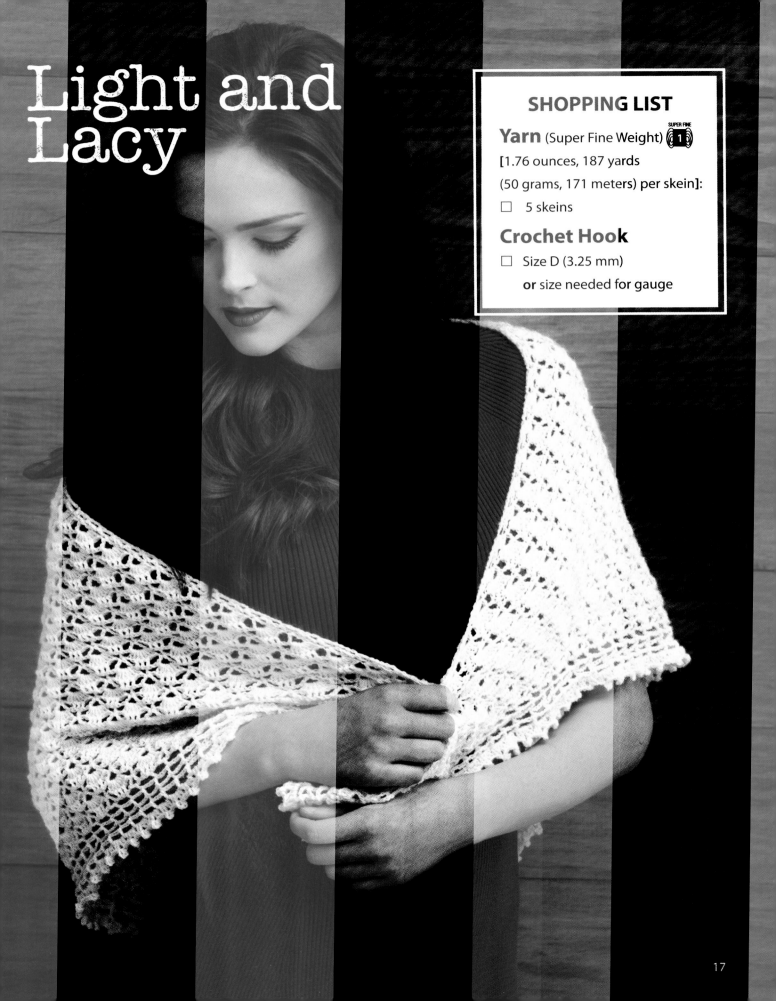

Light and Lacy

Finished Size: 56" wide x 26" deep (142 cm x 66 cm)

 **EASY**

GAUGE INFORMATION

Gauge Swatch: 7" wide x 3½" high
(17.75 cm x 9 cm)

Work same as Wrap through Row 8: 58 sts and 17 sps.

STITCH GUIDE

TREBLE CROCHET (*abbreviated tr*)
YO twice, insert hook in sp indicated, YO and pull up a loop (4 loops on hook), (YO and draw through 2 loops on hook) 3 times.

WRAP

Row 1: Beginning at top edge, use an adjustable loop to form a ring (*Figs. 1a-d, page 30*), ch 5 (**counts as first tr plus ch 1, now and throughout**), (3 dc, ch 3, 3 dc, ch 1, tr in ring: 8 sts and 3 sps.

Row 2 (Right side)**:** Ch 5, turn; dc in next ch-1 sp, ch 1, skip next dc, dc in next dc, ch 1, (3 dc, ch 3, 3 dc) in next ch-3 sp (corner ch-3 sp made), ch 1, skip next dc, dc in next dc, ch 1, (dc, ch 1, tr) in last ch-1 sp, leave last tr unworked (**now and throughout**): 12 sts and 7 sps.

Row 3: Ch 5, turn; dc in next ch-1 sp, ch 1, skip next dc, (dc, ch 3, dc) in next dc, ch 1, skip next ch-1 sp, (3 dc, ch 3, 3 dc) in next corner ch-3 sp, ch 1, skip next 3 dc and next ch-1 sp, (dc, ch 3, dc) in next dc, ch 1, (dc, ch 1, tr) in last ch-1 sp: 14 sts and 9 sps.

Row 4: Ch 5, turn; dc in next ch-1 sp, ch 1, skip next ch-1 sp, 7 dc in next ch-3 sp, ch 1, dc in next ch-1 sp, ch 1, (3 dc, ch 3, 3 dc) in next corner ch-3 sp, ch 1, dc in next ch-1 sp, ch 1, 7 dc in next ch-3 sp, ch 1, skip next ch-1 sp, (dc, ch 1, tr) in last ch-1 sp: 26 sts and 9 sps.

Row 5: Ch 5, turn; dc in next ch-1 sp, ch 1, † (dc, ch 3, dc) in next dc, ch 1, skip next ch-1 sp and next 2 dc, dc in next 3 dc, ch 1, skip next ch-1 sp, (dc, ch 3, dc) in next dc, ch 1 †, skip next ch-1 sp, (3 dc, ch 3, 3 dc) in next corner ch-3 sp, ch 1, skip next ch-1 sp, repeat from † to † once, (dc, ch 1, tr) in last ch-1 sp: 24 sts and 15 sps.

Row 6: Ch 5, turn; dc in next ch-1 sp, ch 1, skip next ch-1 sp, † 7 dc in next ch-3 sp, ch 1, skip next ch-1 sp and next dc, dc in next dc, ch 1, skip next ch-1 sp, 7 dc in next ch-3 sp, ch 1 †, dc in next ch-1 sp, ch 1, (3 dc, ch 3, 3 dc) in next corner ch-3 sp, ch 1, dc in next ch-1 sp, ch 1, repeat from † to † once, skip next ch-1 sp, (dc, ch 1, tr) in last ch-1 sp: 42 sts and 13 sps.

Row 7: Ch 5, turn; dc in next ch-1 sp, ch 1, (dc, ch 3, dc) in next dc, † ch 1, skip next ch-1 sp and next 2 dc, dc in next 3 dc, ch 1, skip next ch-1 sp, (dc, ch 3, dc) in next dc †; repeat from † to † across to within one ch-1 sp of next corner ch-3 sp, ch 1, skip ch-1 sp, (3 dc, ch 3, 3 dc) in corner ch-3 sp, ch 1, skip next ch-1 sp, (dc, ch 3, dc) in next dc, repeat from † to † across to last ch-1 sp, ch 1, (dc, ch 1, tr) in last ch-1 sp: 34 sts and 21 sps.

Row 8: Ch 5, turn; dc in next ch-1 sp, ch 1, skip next ch-1 sp, 7 dc in next ch-3 sp, ch 1, † skip next ch-1 sp and next dc, dc in next dc, ch 1, skip next ch-1 sp, 7 dc in next ch-3 sp, ch 1 †; repeat from † to † across to within one ch-1 sp of next corner ch-3 sp, dc in ch-1 sp, ch 1, (3 dc, ch 3, 3 dc) in corner ch-3 sp, ch 1, dc in next ch-1 sp, ch 1, 7 dc in next ch-3 sp, repeat from † to † across to last 2 ch-1 sps, skip next ch-1 sp, (dc, ch 1, tr) in last ch-1 sp: 58 sts and 17 sps.

BOTTOM EDGING

Row 1: Ch 6 (**counts as first tr plus ch 2, now and throughout**), turn; dc in next ch-1 sp, † ch 4, skip next ch-1 sp, dc in next ch-3 sp, ch 4, skip next ch-1 sp and next dc, dc in next dc †; repeat from † to † across to next corner ch-3 sp, ch 2, (dc, ch 2) twice in corner ch-3 sp, skip next dc, dc in next dc, repeat from † to † across to last 4 sps, ch 4, skip next ch-1 sp, dc in next ch-3 sp, ch 4, skip next ch-1 sp, (dc, ch 2, tr) in last ch-1 sp.

Repeat Rows 7 and 8 for pattern until piece measures approximately 52" (132 cm) across top edge, ending by working Row 7; at end of last row, do **not** finish off.

Rows 2-4: Ch 6, turn; dc in next ch-2 sp, (ch 4, skip next ch-4 sp, dc in next dc) across to next ch-2 sp, ch 4, skip ch-2 sp, dc in next dc, ch 2, (dc, ch 2) twice in next corner ch-2 sp, dc in next dc, ch 4, skip next ch-2 sp, dc in next dc, ch 4, (skip next ch-4 sp, dc in next dc, ch 4) across to last ch-2 sp, (dc, ch 2, tr) in last ch-2 sp.

Row 5: Ch 1, turn; (2 dc, ch 4, slip st in third ch from hook, ch 1, 2 dc) in next sp and in each sp across; finish off.

Yarn (Light Weight) 🧶**3**
[2.6 ounces, 173 yards
(75 grams, 158 meters) per skein]:
☐ 3 skeins

Crochet Hook
☐ Size J (6 mm)
   or size needed for gauge

Lacy Triangle

Finished Size: 60" wide (across top edge) x 19½" deep
(152.5 cm x 49.5 cm)

 ●●○○ **EASY**

GAUGE INFORMATION

In pattern,

2 repeats (10 sts and 5 sps) = 4¾" (12 cm);

5 rows = 2¾" (7 cm)

Gauge Swatch: 5" wide x 2¾" high

(12.75 cm x 7 cm)

Ch 23.

Rows 1-3: Work same as Shawl: 11 sts and 8 sps.

Row 4: Ch 5 **(counts as first dc plus ch 2)**, turn; † sc in next ch-3 sp, ch 2, 3 dc in next dc, ch 2, sc in next ch-3 sp †, ch 5, skip next ch-1 sp, repeat from † to † once, ch 2, dc in last tr.

Row 5: Ch 1, turn; sc in first dc, ch 3, skip next sc, dc in next dc, (ch 1, dc in next dc) twice, ch 3, skip next ch-2 sp, sc in next ch-5 sp, ch 3, skip next ch-2 sp, dc in next dc, (ch 1, dc in next dc) twice, ch 3, skip next ch-2 sp, sc in last ch-2 sp, leave last dc unworked: 9 sts and 8 sps.

Finish off.

STITCH GUIDE

TREBLE CROCHET *(abbreviated tr)*

YO twice, insert hook in st indicated, YO and pull a loop (4 loops on hook), (YO and draw through 2 loops on hook) 3 times.

WRAP

Ch 207, place marker in fifth ch from hook for st placement.

Row 1 (Right side)**:** Sc in eighth ch from hook **(first 5 skipped chs count as first dc plus ch 2)**, ch 2, skip next ch, 3 dc in next ch, ch 2, skip next ch, sc in next ch, ★ ch 5, skip next 3 chs, sc in next ch, ch 2, skip next ch, 3 dc in next ch, ch 2, skip next ch, sc in next ch; repeat from ★ across to last 3 chs, ch 2, skip next 2 chs, dc in last ch: 127 sts and 76 sps.

Note: Loop a short piece of yarn around any stitch to mark Row 1 as **right** side.

Row 2: Ch 1, turn; sc in first dc, ch 3, skip next sc, dc in next dc, (ch 1, dc in next dc) twice, ch 3, ★ skip next ch-2 sp, sc in next ch-5 sp, ch 3, skip next ch-2 sp, dc in next dc, (ch 1, dc in next dc) twice, ch 3; repeat from ★ across to last 2 ch-2 sps, skip next ch-2 sp, sc in last ch-2 sp, leave last dc unworked: 101 sts and 100 sps.

Row 3: Ch 4 **(counts as first tr, now and throughout)**, turn; dc in next dc, (ch 3, dc in next dc) twice, ★ ch 1, skip next sc, dc in next dc, (ch 3, dc in next dc) twice; repeat from ★ across to last sc, tr in last sc: 77 sts and 74 sps.

Row 4 (Decrease row): Turn; slip st in first tr and in next dc, (slip st in next 3 chs and in next dc) twice, slip st in next ch-1 sp, ch 5 **(counts as first dc plus ch 2, now and throughout)**, skip next dc, sc in next ch-3 sp, ch 2, 3 dc in next dc, ch 2, sc in next ch-3 sp, ★ ch 5, skip next ch-1 sp, sc in next ch-3 sp, ch 2, 3 dc in next dc, ch 2, sc in next ch-3 sp; repeat from ★ across to last 3 sps, ch 2, dc in next ch-1 sp, leave remaining 2 sps unworked: 117 sts and 70 sps.

Row 5: Ch 1, turn; sc in first dc, ch 3, skip next 2 ch-2 sps, dc in next dc, (ch 1, dc in next dc) twice, ch 3, ★ skip next ch-2 sp, sc in next ch-5 sp, ch 3, skip next ch-2 sp, dc in next dc, (ch 1, dc in next dc) twice, ch 3; repeat from ★ across to last 2 ch-2 sps, skip next ch-2 sp, sc in last ch-2 sp, leave last dc unworked: 93 sts and 92 sps.

Row 6: Ch 4, turn; dc in next dc, (ch 3, dc in next dc) twice, ★ ch 1, skip next sc, dc in next dc, (ch 3, dc in next dc) twice; repeat from ★ across to last ch-3 sp, skip last ch-3 sp, tr in last sc: 71 sts and 68 sps.

Rows 7-36: Repeat Rows 4-6, 10 times: 11 sts and 8 sps.

Row 37: Turn; slip st in first tr and in next dc, (slip st in next 3 chs and in next dc) twice, slip st in next ch-1 sp, ch 5, skip next dc, sc in next ch-3 sp, ch 2, 3 dc in next dc, ch 2, sc in next ch-3 sp, ch 2, dc in next ch-1 sp, leave remaining 2 sps unworked: 7 sts and 4 ch-2 sps.

Row 38: Ch 1, turn; sc in first dc, ch 3, skip next sc, dc in next dc, (ch 1, dc in next dc) twice, ch 3, sc in last ch-2 sp, leave last dc unworked: 5 sts and 4 sps.

Row 39: Ch 4, turn; dc in next dc, (ch 3, dc in next dc) twice, skip last ch-3 sp, tr in last sc; finish off.

Edging: With **right** side facing and working in free loops *(Fig. 2, page 30)* and in sps across beginning ch, join yarn with sc in ch at base of last dc *(see Joining With Sc, page 30)*; 2 sc in next ch-2 sp, skip next ch, sc in next sp and in next ch at base of 3-dc group, sc in next sp, ★ skip next ch, 3 sc in next sp, skip next ch, sc in next sp and in next ch at base of next 3-dc group, sc in next sp; repeat from ★ across within 3 chs of marked ch, skip next ch, 2 sc in next ch-2 sp, sc in marked ch, remove marker; sc evenly across to Row 39; sc in first tr, skip next dc, (3 sc in next ch-3 sp, skip next dc) twice, sc in last tr; sc evenly across; join with slip st to first sc, finish off.

Shawlette

Finished Size: 68" long x 10½" wide (172.5 cm x 26.5 cm)

 **EASY**

GAUGE INFORMATION

18 dc and 8 rows = 4" (10 cm)

Gauge Swatch: 4" (10 cm) square

Ch 20.

Row 1: Dc in fourth ch from hook (**3 skipped chs count as first dc**) and in each ch across: 18 dc.

Rows 2-8: Ch 3 (**counts as first dc**), turn; dc in next dc and in each dc across.

Finish off.

STITCH GUIDE

DOUBLE CROCHET 2 TOGETHER

(abbreviated dc2tog) (uses next 2 dc)

★ YO, insert hook in **next** dc, YO and pull up a loop, YO and draw through 2 loops on hook; repeat from ★ once **more**, YO and draw through all 3 loops on hook (**counts as one dc**).

WRAP

Ch 13, place marker in third ch from hook for st placement.

Row 1: Dc in eighth ch from hook and in next ch, ch 3, skip next 3 chs, 4 dc in last ch: 6 dc and 2 sps.

Row 2 (Right side)**:** Ch 3, turn; slip st in first dc, ch 2, hdc in next dc, ch 2, hdc in next 2 dc, ch 3, dc in next 2 dc, ch 2, 2 dc in marked ch, remove marker: 7 sts and 5 sps.

Row 3: Ch 3 (**counts as first dc**), turn; dc in next dc, ch 2, dc in next 2 dc, ch 3, skip next ch-3 sp, (3 dc, ch 1, 3 dc) in next ch-2 sp, leave remaining sts unworked: 10 dc and 3 sps.

Row 4: Ch 3, turn; slip st in first dc, ch 2, hdc in next 2 dc, ch 2, hdc in next 3 dc, ch 3, dc in next 2 dc, ch 2, dc in next dc, 2 dc in last dc: 10 sts and 5 sps.

Row 5: Ch 3 (**counts as first dc**), turn; dc in next 2 dc, ch 2, dc in next 2 dc, ch 3, skip next ch-3 sp, (3 dc, ch 1, 3 dc) in next ch-2 sp, leave remaining sts unworked: 11 dc and 3 sps.

Row 6: Ch 3, turn; slip st in first dc, ch 2, hdc in next 2 dc, ch 2, hdc in next 3 dc, ch 3, dc in next 2 dc, ch 2, dc in next 2 dc, 2 dc in last dc: 11 sts and 5 sps.

Row 7: Ch 3 (**counts as first dc**), turn; dc in next dc and in each dc across to next ch-2 sp, ch 2, dc in next 2 dc, ch 3, skip next ch-3 sp, (3 dc, ch 1, 3 dc) in next ch-2 sp, leave remaining sts unworked: 12 dc and 3 sps.

Row 8 (Increase row)**:** Ch 3, turn; slip st in first dc, ch 2, hdc in next 2 dc, ch 2, hdc in next 3 dc, ch 3, dc in next 2 dc, ch 2, dc in next dc and in each dc across to last dc, 2 dc in last dc: 12 sts and 5 sps.

Rows 9-69: Repeat Rows 7 and 8, 30 times; then repeat Row 7 once **more**: 43 dc and 3 sps.

Row 70 (Decrease row): Ch 3, turn; slip st in first dc, ch 2, hdc in next 2 dc, ch 2, hdc in next 3 dc, ch 3, dc in next 2 dc, ch 2, dc in next dc and in each dc across to last 2 dc, dc2tog: 41 sts and 5 sps.

Row 71: Ch 3 (**counts as first dc**), turn; dc in next dc and in each dc across to next ch-2 sp, ch 2, dc in next 2 dc, ch 3, (3 dc, ch 1, 3 dc) in next ch-2 sp, leave remaining sts unworked: 42 dc and 3 sps.

Rows 72-135: Repeat Rows 70 and 71, 32 times: 10 dc and 3 sps.

Row 136: Ch 3, turn; slip st in first dc, ch 2, hdc in next 2 dc, ch 2, hdc in next 3 dc, ch 3, dc in next 2 dc, ch 2, dc2tog; finish off.

SHOPPING LIST

Yarn (Fine Weight) 🧶**2**
[3.5 ounces, 317 yards
(100 grams, 290 meters) per skein]:
☐ 5 skeins

Crochet Hook
☐ Size G (4 mm)
  or size needed for gauge

Leafy Lacework

Finished Size: 68½" long x 25" wide (174 cm x 63.5 cm)

●●○○ **EASY**

GAUGE INFORMATION

In pattern,

8 dc and 4 ch-2 sps (one repeat) = 3¼" (8.25 cm);

7 rows = 3" (7.5 cm)

Gauge Swatch: 6¾" wide x 3" high

(17.25 cm x 7.5 cm)

Ch 37.

Work same as Wrap through Row 7: 17 dc and

8 ch-2 sps.

Finish off.

STITCH GUIDE

DOUBLE CROCHET 2 TOGETHER

(abbreviated dc2tog) (uses next 2 dc)

★ YO, insert hook in **next** dc, YO and pull up a loop,
YO and draw through 2 loops on hook; repeat from
★ once **more**, YO and draw through all 3 loops on
hook (**counts as one dc**).

DOUBLE CROCHET 3 TOGETHER

(abbreviated dc3tog) (uses next 3 dc)

★ YO, insert hook in **next** dc, YO and pull up a loop,
YO and draw through 2 loops on hook; repeat from
★ 2 times **more**, YO and draw through all 4 loops on
hook (**counts as one dc**).

WRAP

Ch 341, place marker in fifth ch from hook for
st placement.

Row 1 (Right side)**:** Dc in eighth ch from hook, ch 2,
skip next 2 chs, dc in next 5 chs, ★ (ch 2, skip next 2 chs,
dc in next ch) 3 times, ch 2, skip next 2 chs, dc in next
5 chs; repeat from ★ across to last 6 chs, (ch 2, skip next
2 chs, dc in next ch) twice: 169 sts and 84 sps.

Row 2: Ch 3 (**counts as first dc, now and throughout**),
turn; dc in first dc, ch 2, dc in next dc, ch 2, dc2tog, dc
in next dc, dc2tog, ch 2, dc in next dc, ch 2, ★ 3 dc in
next dc, ch 2, dc in next dc, ch 2, dc2tog, dc in next dc,
dc2tog, ch 2, dc in next dc, ch 2; repeat from ★ across
to last sp, skip next 2 chs, 2 dc in next ch: 169 dc and
84 ch-2 sps.

Row 3: Ch 3, turn; ★ 2 dc in next dc, ch 2, dc in next dc,
ch 2, dc3tog, ch 2, dc in next dc, ch 2, 2 dc in next dc, dc
in next dc; repeat from ★ across.

Row 4: Ch 3, turn; dc in next 2 dc, ch 2, (dc in next dc,
ch 2) 3 times, ★ dc in next 5 dc, ch 2, (dc in next dc,
ch 2) 3 times; repeat from ★ across to last 3 dc, dc in last
3 dc.

Row 5: Ch 3, turn; ★ dc2tog, ch 2, dc in next dc, ch 2,
3 dc in next dc, ch 2, dc in next dc, ch 2, dc2tog, dc in
next dc; repeat from ★ across.

Row 6: Ch 2 (**does not count as a st**), turn; dc in next dc, ch 2, dc in next dc, ch 2, 2 dc in next dc, dc in next dc, 2 dc in next dc, ch 2, dc in next dc, ch 2, ★ dc3tog, ch 2, dc in next dc, ch 2, 2 dc in next dc, dc in next dc, 2 dc in next dc, ch 2, dc in next dc, ch 2; repeat from ★ across to last 2 dc, dc2tog.

Row 7: Ch 5 (**counts as first dc plus ch 2**), turn; dc in next dc, ch 2, dc in next 5 dc, ch 2, ★ (dc in next dc, ch 2) 3 times, dc in next 5 dc, ch 2; repeat from ★ across to last 2 dc, dc in next dc, ch 2, dc in last dc.

Repeat Rows 2-7 for pattern until piece measures approximately 24½" (62 cm) from beginning ch, ending by working Row 7; at end of last row, do **not** finish off.

EDGING

Rnd 1: Ch 1, do **not** turn; sc evenly across ends of rows to beginning ch; working in free loops (**Fig. 2, page 30**) and in sps across beginning ch, 3 sc in first ch, † 2 sc in next ch-2 sp, sc in next st, 2 sc in next ch-2 sp, sc in next 5 sts, 2 sc in next ch-2 sp, ★ (sc in next st, 2 sc in next ch-2 sp) 3 times, sc in next 5 sts, 2 sc in next ch-2 sp; repeat from ★ across to last ch-2 sp, sc in next st, 2 sc in last ch-2 sp †, 3 sc in marked ch, remove marker; sc evenly across ends of rows; working in sts across last row, 3 sc in first dc, repeat from † to † once, 3 sc in last dc; join with slip st to first sc.

Rnd 2: Ch 1, working from **left** to **right**, work reverse sc in each sc around (**Figs. A-D**); join with slip st to first st, finish off.

REVERSE SINGLE CROCHET (abbreviated reverse sc)

Working from **left** to **right**, ★ insert hook in st to right of hook (**Fig. A**), YO and draw through, under and to left of loop on hook (2 loops on hook) (**Fig. B**), YO and draw through both loops on hook (**Fig. C**) (**reverse sc made, Fig. D**); repeat from ★ around.

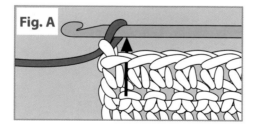

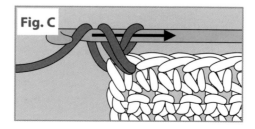

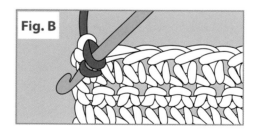

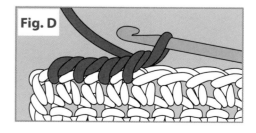

General Instructions

ABBREVIATIONS

ch(s)	chain(s)
cm	centimeters
dc	double crochet(s)
dc2tog	double crochet 2 together
dc3tog	double crochet 3 together
hdc	half double crochet(s)
mm	millimeters
Rnd(s)	Round(s)
sc	single crochet(s)
sp(s)	space(s)
st(s)	stitch(es)
tr	treble crochet(s)
YO	yarn over

SYMBOLS & TERMS

★ — work instructions following ★ as many **more** times as indicated in addition **to** the first time.

† to † — work all instructions from first † to second † **as many** times as specified.

( ) or [ ] — work enclosed instructions **as many** times as specified by the number immediately following **or** work all enclosed instructions in the stitch or space indicated **or** contains explanatory remarks.

colon (:) — the number(s) given after a colon at the end of a row or round denote(s) the number of stitches or spaces you should have on that row or round.

CROCHET TERMINOLOGY

UNITED STATES		INTERNATIONAL
slip stitch (slip st)	=	single crochet (sc)
single crochet (sc)	=	double crochet (dc)
half double crochet (hdc)	=	half treble crochet (htr)
double crochet (dc)	=	treble crochet (tr)
treble crochet (tr)	=	double treble crochet (dtr)
double treble crochet (dtr)	=	triple treble crochet (ttr)
triple treble crochet (tr tr)	=	quadruple treble crochet (qtr)
skip	=	miss

●○○○ BEGINNER	Projects for first-time crocheters using basic stitches. Minimal shaping.
●●○○ EASY	Projects using yarn with basic stitches, repetitive stitch patterns, simple color changes, and simple shaping and finishing.
●●●○ INTERMEDIATE	Projects using a variety of techniques, such as basic lace patterns or color patterns, mid-level shaping and finishing.
●●●● EXPERIENCED	Projects with intricate stitch patterns, techniques and dimension, such as non-repeating patterns, multi-color techniques, fine threads, small hooks, detailed shaping and refined finishing.

CROCHET HOOKS																
U.S.	B-1	C-2	D-3	E-4	F-5	G-6	7	H-8	I-9	J-10	K-10½	L-11	M/N-13	N/P-15	P/Q	Q	S
Metric - mm	2.25	2.75	3.25	3.5	3.75	4	4.5	5	5.5	6	6.5	8	9	10	15	16	19

GAUGE

Exact gauge is **essential** for proper size. Before beginning your project, make the sample swatch given in the individual instructions in the yarn and hook specified. After completing the swatch, measure it, counting your stitches and rows carefully. If your swatch is larger or smaller than specified, **make another, changing hook size to get the correct gauge**. Keep trying until you find the size hook that will give you the specified gauge.

JOINING WITH SC

When instructed to join with sc, begin with a slip knot on hook. Insert hook in stitch or space indicated, YO and pull up a loop, YO and draw through both loops on hook.

ADJUSTABLE LOOP

Wind yarn around two fingers to form a ring *(Fig. 1a)*. Slide yarn off fingers and grasp the strands at the top of the ring *(Fig. 1b)*. Insert hook from **front** to **back** into the ring, pull up a loop, YO and draw through loop on hook to lock ring *(Fig. 1c)* (st made does **not** count as part of beginning ch). Working around both strands, follow instructions to work sts in the ring, then pull yarn tail to close *(Fig. 1d)*.

FREE LOOPS OF A CHAIN

When instructed to work in free loops of a chain, work in loop indicated by arrow *(Fig. 2)*.

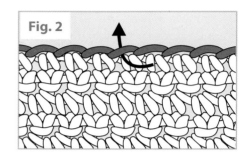

CHANGING COLORS

Work the last stitch to within one step of completion, hook new yarn *(Fig. 3)* and draw through all loops on hook.

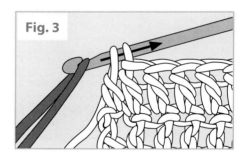

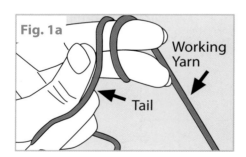

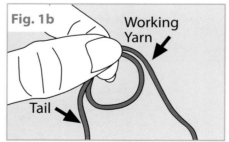

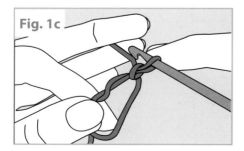

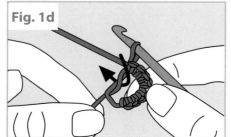

Yarn Information

The Wraps in this book were made using a variety of yarn weights. Any brand of the specific weight of yarn may be used. It is best to refer to the yardage/meters when determining how many balls or skeins to purchase. Remember, to achieve the same look, it is the weight of yarn that is important, not the brand of yarn.

For your convenience, listed below are the specific yarns used to create our photography models. Because yarn manufacturers make frequent changes in their product lines, you may sometimes find it necessary to use a substitute yarn or to search for the discontinued product at alternate suppliers (locally or online).

SPARKLE

Red Heart® Swanky™

#9522 Tealessence

SHIMMERING RIPPLE

Lion Brand® Vanna's Glamour®

Purple - #145 Purple Topaz

Wine - #189 Garnet

Lt Grey - #150 Platinum

Lion Brand® Vanna's Complement®

Grey - #151 Charcoal Grey

STEPPING OUT

Lion Brand® 24/7 Cotton

Grey - #150 Charcoal

Blue - #108 Denim

Lt Blue - #107 Sky

Lt Grey - #149 Silver

Ecru - #098 Ecru

PRETTY PICOTS

Lion Brand® Vanna's Style

Teal - #178 Teal

Brown - #125 Taupe

Red - #134 Tomato

LIGHT AND LACY

Red Heart® Heart & Sole®

#3313 Ivory

LACY TRIANGLE

Lion Brand® Modern Baby®

#149 Grey

SHAWLETTE

Red Heart® Unforgettable®

#3952 Tealberry

LEAFY LACEWORK

Premier Yarn® Cotton Fair™

#27-16 Cocoa

Yarn Weight Symbol & Names	LACE (0)	SUPER FINE (1)	FINE (2)	LIGHT (3)	MEDIUM (4)	BULKY (5)	SUPER BULKY (6)	JUMBO (7)
Type of Yarns in Category	Fingering, size 10 crochet thread	Sock, Fingering, Baby	Sport, Baby	DK, Light Worsted	Worsted, Afghan, Aran	Chunky, Craft, Rug	Super Bulky, Roving	Jumbo, Roving
Crochet Gauge* Ranges in Single Crochet to 4" (10 cm)	32-42 sts**	21-32 sts	16-20 sts	12-17 sts	11-14 sts	8-11 sts	6-9 sts	5 sts and fewer
Advised Hook Size Range	Steel*** 6 to 8, Regular hook B-1	B-1 to E-4	E-4 to 7	7 to I-9	I-9 to K-10½	K-10½ to M/N-13	M/N-13 to Q	Q and larger

*GUIDELINES ONLY: The chart above reflects the most commonly used gauges and hook sizes for specific yarn categories.

** Lace weight yarns are usually crocheted with larger hooks to create lacy openwork patterns. Accordingly, a gauge range is difficult to determine. Always follow the gauge stated in your pattern.

*** Steel crochet hooks are sized differently from regular hooks–the higher the number, the smaller the hook, which is the reverse of regular hook sizing.

Meet the Designer:
Melissa Leapman

With more than 800 knit and crochet designs in print, Melissa Leapman is one of the most widely published American designers working today.

She began her design career by freelancing for leading ready-to-wear design houses in New York City. She also created designs to help top yarn companies promote their new and existing yarns each season. Her ability to quickly develop fully envisioned garments put her skills in great demand.

Through the years, Leisure Arts has published more than 40 books of Melissa's fabulous designs. Melissa is also the host of several Leisure Arts DVDs in the best-selling teach-yourself series, "I Can't Believe I'm Knitting" and "I Can't Believe I'm Crocheting."

Nationally, her designs have been featured in numerous magazines, and her workshops on knitting and crochet are consistently popular with crafters of all skill levels. She has taught at major events such as STITCHES, Vogue Knitting LIVE, and The Knitting Guild Association conferences, as well as at hundreds of yarn shops and local guild events across the country.

To find more of Melissa's designs, visit LeisureArts.com, Melissa's Facebook page, and Ravelry.com.

We have made every effort to ensure that these instructions are accurate and complete. We cannot, however, be responsible for human error, typographical mistakes, or variations in individual work.

Production Team: Instructional/Technical Editor - Sarah J. Green; Editorial Writer - Susan Frantz Wiles; Senior Graphic Artist - Lora Puls; Graphic Artist - Leia Morshedi; Photo Stylist - Lori Wenger; and Photographer - Jason Masters.

Instructions tested and photo models made by Janet Akins, Amanda Loggins, Barbara Schou, and Stacey Williams.